HOO, WHO'S TI

A KNOCK-KNOCK JOKE IN RHYTHM AND RHYME

By BLAKE HOENA

Illustrated by KLAUS BIPPER

Music Produced by ERIK KOSKINEN and
Recorded at REAL PHONIC STUDIOS

CANTATA
LEARNING

WWW.CANTATALEARNING.COM

CANTATA
LEARNING

Published by Cantata Learning
1710 Roe Crest Drive
North Mankato, MN 56003
www.cantatalearning.com

A note to educators and librarians from the publisher: Cantata Learning has provided the following data to assist in book processing and suggested use of Cantata Learning product.

Publisher's Cataloging-in-Publication Data
Prepared by Librarian Consultant: Ann-Marie Begnaud
Library of Congress Control Number: 2015958175
    Hoo, Who's There? : A Knock-Knock Joke in Rhythm and Rhyme
    Series: Jokes and Jingles
    By Blake Hoena
    Illustrated by Klaus Bipper
    Summary: Rhythmic music is paired with a graphic novel format to tell this classic knock-knock joke.
    ISBN: 978-1-63290-620-5 (library binding/CD)
    ISBN: 978-1-63290-632-8 (paperback/CD)
Suggested Dewey and Subject Headings:
    Dewey: E 818.602
    LCSH Subject Headings: Biotic communities – Juvenile humor. | Biotic communities – Songs and music – Texts. | Biotic communities – Juvenile sound recordings.
    Sears Subject Headings: Jokes. | Ecology – humor. | School songbooks. | Children's songs. | Jazz music.
    BISAC Subject Headings: JUVENILE NONFICTION / Humor / Jokes & Riddles. | JUVENILE NONFICTION / Music / Songbooks. | JUVENILE NONFICTION / Science & Nature / Environmental Science & Ecosystems.

Book design and art direction, Tim Palin Creative
Editorial direction, Flat Sole Studio
Music direction, Elizabeth Draper
Music produced by Erik Koskinen and recorded at Real Phonic Studios

Printed in the United States of America in North Mankato, Minnesota.
072016   0335CGF16

As Peter the squirrel **scampers** through the forest, he sees different animal homes. There is a **den**, a **burrow**, a **hive**, and a nest. Peter wants to find his friend the owl, so he knocks on each one.

To find out who's there,
turn the page and sing along!

Scampering through the woods one day,
Peter was off to find his friend.

He looked around and found a cave that he thought was somebody's den.

Who.

Who, who?

But wolves don't hoot. They howl.

Ar-ar-ar-rooooooo!

"So sorry," Peter sang and quickly ran away.

He looked up high, and he searched down low.
He sniffed the ground and watched the sky.

Then he spotted, up in a tree,
hanging from a branch, a beehive.

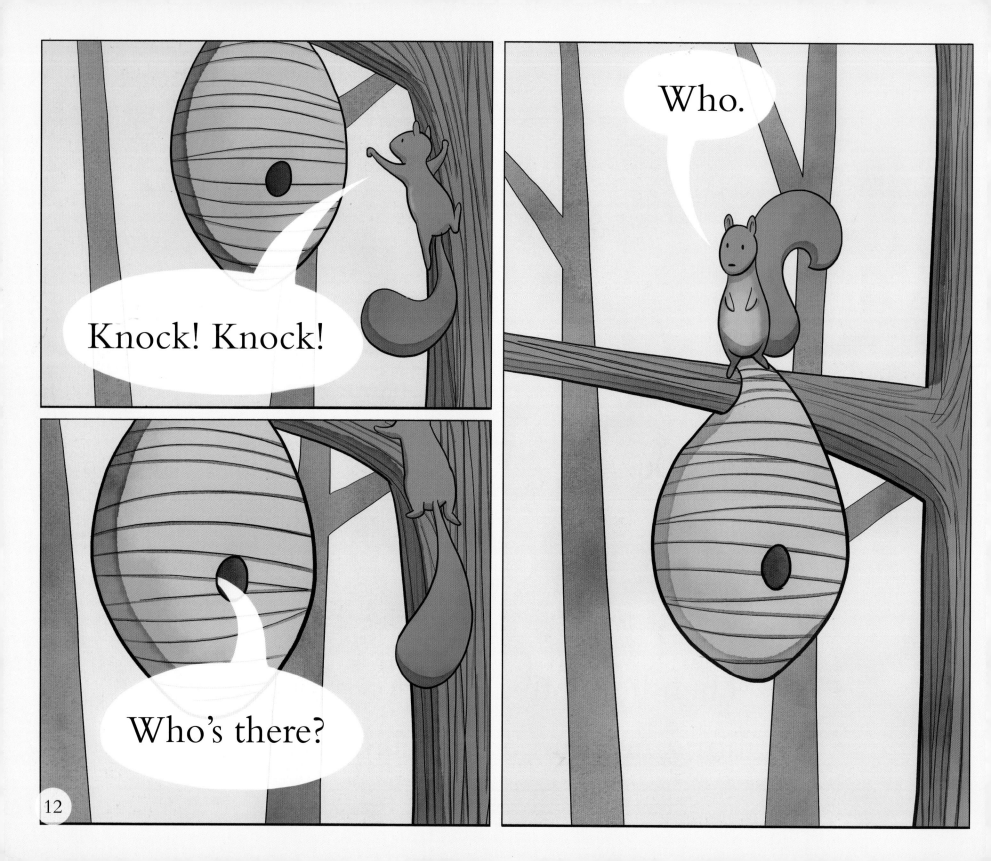

13

Through the woods, up in mountains,
down in **grasslands**, and all around,

he searched and searched,
until he found
a deep hole leading underground.

16

But snakes don't hoot.
They hiss.

Hiss-hiss-hissssss.

"So sorry," Peter sang
and quickly ran away.

Peter felt sad and all alone.
He was about to give up hope.

But then, throughout the woods, he heard, "Hoo, who! Hoo, who!" from a tree hole.

It's me, Ollie.

That's who! Hoo, who!

"So happy I found you," Peter sang, and they ran off to play.

SONG LYRICS
Hoo, Who's There?

Knock! Knock!

Scampering through the woods one day,
Peter was off to find his friend.

He looked around and found a cave
that he thought was somebody's den.

Knock! Knock!
Who's there?
Who.
Who, who?

But wolves don't hoot.
They howl. Ar-ar-ar-rooooooo!

"So sorry," Peter sang
and quickly ran away.

He looked up high, and he searched down low.
He sniffed the ground and watched the sky.

Then he spotted, up in a tree,
hanging from a branch, a beehive.

Knock! Knock!
Who's there?
Who.
Who, who?

But bees don't hoot.
They buzz. Buzz-buzz-buzzzzzzzzz!

"So sorry," Peter sang
and quickly ran away.

Through the woods, up in mountains,
down in grasslands, and all around,

he searched and searched, until he found
a deep hole leading underground.

Knock! Knock!
Who's there?
Who.
Who, who?

But snakes don't hoot.
They hiss. Hiss-hiss-hissssssss.

"So sorry," Peter sang
and quickly ran away.

Peter felt sad and all alone.
He was about to give up hope.

But then, throughout the woods, he heard,
"Hoo, who! Hoo, who!" from a tree hole.

Knock! Knock!
Who's there?
Who.
Who, who?

It's me, Ollie.
That's who! Hoo, who!

"So happy I found you," Peter sang,
and they ran off to play.

Who's there?

Hoo, Who's There?

Americana
Erik Koskinen

Verse

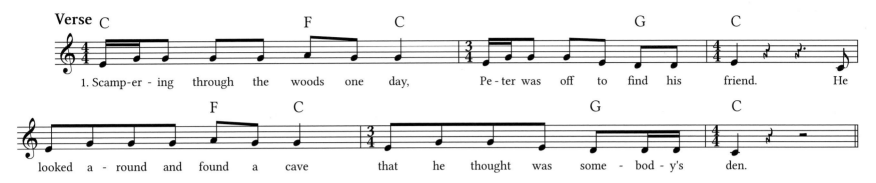

1. Scamp-er - ing through the woods one day, Pe - ter was off to find his friend. He
looked a - round and found a cave that he thought was some - bod - y's den.

Chorus

Knock! Knock! Who's there? Who. Who, who? But wolves don't hoot. They howl.

Ar - ar - ar-rooooooo! "So sor - ry," Pe - ter sang and quick - ly ran a - way.

Verse 2
He looked up high, and he searched down low.
He sniffed the ground and watched the sky.
Then he spotted, up in a tree,
hanging from a branch, a beehive.

Chorus
Knock! Knock! Who's there?
Who. Who, who?
But bees don't hoot.
They buzz. Buzz-buzz-buzzzzzzzz!
"So sorry," Peter sang
and quickly ran away.

Verse 3
Through the woods, up in mountains,
down in grasslands, and all around,
he searched and searched, until he found
a deep hole leading underground.

Chorus
Knock! Knock! Who's there?
Who. Who, who?
But snakes don't hoot.
They hiss. Hiss-hiss-hisssssss.
"So sorry," Peter sang
and quickly ran away.

Verse 4
Peter felt sad and all alone.
He was about to give up hope.
But then, throughout the woods, he heard,
"Hoo, who! Hoo, who!" from a tree hole.

Chorus
Knock! Knock! Who's there?
Who. Who, who?
It's me, Ollie.
That's who! Hoo, who!
"So happy I found you," Peter sang,
and they ran off to play.

GLOSSARY

burrow—a hole dug in the ground by a small animal

den—the home of a wild animal

grasslands—large, open areas of grass

hive—a nest or house for a swarm of bees

scampers—runs

GUIDED READING ACTIVITIES

1. In this story, you see Peter the squirrel climbing, jumping, and sitting in a tree. Draw a picture of a tree. Now draw a squirrel in your tree.

2. Peter wanted to play with his friend Ollie the Owl. What do you like to do with your friends?

3. In this story, Peter visits several animal homes. What other animals might live in one of these homes, such as a beehive, a den, or a hole in the ground?

TO LEARN MORE

Anderson, Steven. *The More We Get Together*. North Mankato, MN: Cantata Learning, 2016.

Barna, Tom David. *Who Lives in a Tree? A Song about Where Animals Live*. Minneapolis, MN: Cantata Learning, 2016.

De la Bédoyère, Camilla. *The Wild Life of Owls*. New York: Windmill Books, 2015.

Marsh, Laura. *Owls*. Washington, DC: National Geographic, 2014.